Gate of Lilacs

ALSO BY CLIVE JAMES

CLIVE JAMES

Gate of Lilacs

A Verse Commentary on Proust

PICADOR

First published 2016 by Picador
an imprint of Pan Macmillan
20 New Wharf Road, London N1 9RR
Associated companies throughout the world
www.panmacmillan.com

ISBN 978-1-5098-1235-6

1 3 5 7 9 8 6 4 2

A CIP catalogue record for this book is available from the British Library.

Printed and bound by CPI Group (UK) Ltd, Croydon, CR0 4YY

Visit **www.picador.com** to read more about all our books
and to buy them. You will also find features, author interviews and
news of any author events, and you can sign up for e-newsletters
so that you're always first to hear about our new releases.

to Prue

Et si jamais ma pauvre âme amoureuse
Ne doit avoir de bien en vérité,
Faites au moins qu'elle en ait en mensonge.

Louise Labé

Acknowledgements

Among various friends upon whom I inflicted the manuscript of this poem as it took form, there were several who made specific remarks that I tried to take account of in the later stages of its composition. I should especially acknowledge the critical attention of Stephen Edgar, who combines his excellence as a lyric poet with a professional competence as an editor of texts: in the latter role he kindly agreed to take on the task of seeing my completed manuscript through the press. Deirdre Serjeantson and Adam Gopnik both made me think again about points that I had thought were smoothly covered already. My thanks also to P.J. O'Rourke, Prue Shaw and Tom Stoppard. Above all I must thank Don Paterson at Picador, who gave the project his approval after seeing only the first few sections in their scarcely settled form. He hadn't been expecting to see anything quite like that, but perhaps he was touched by my assurances that I hadn't either. The poem came out of the blue. But poems always do, when you're in luck.

Contents

Introduction

Because I was doing other things, such as earning a living, it took me fifteen years to learn French by almost no other method except reading *A la recherche du temps perdu*, so I was a long time getting to be as familiar with Proust's great novel as most English readers become by reading a translation of it in a few months. Usually they get no further than the first couple of volumes but they are pleased to have made inroads into its frame of reference. They ought to be, in my view. Proust is not a whole world, as is sometimes claimed; but he was unbeatable at taking, for a basic subject, his own small world, the fashionable world in Paris in the late nineteenth and the early twentieth centuries; and then, beyond that, analysing the irrepressible beginnings of the world of art that we all inhabit today, where creative people take first place in the rankings of prestige, and the old nobility come a distant third, somewhere behind ex-KGB billionaires with yachts the size of destroyers.

Leave Proust out and you miss some of the taste of that crucial time. Even while I was taking the long way round, however, I could tell that he was a mighty man, and I took notes in the endpapers of my Livre de Poche volumes as I slogged my way forward, French dictionary in hand. Later on, when I read the great Scott Moncrieff translation, *Remembrance of Things Past*, in order to see where I had been, I made more notes; and then more notes as I read the novel once again in the original, in the beautiful three-volume Pléiade edition; and then back to the English translation as it was augmented first by my dear friend Terence Kilmartin and then by the poet D. J. Enright; and so on. Last of all, after yet another pass through the Pléiade edition, which had itself been augmented to four volumes, I went page by page through *In Search of Lost Time*, the magnificent Modern Library six-volume edition as published in New York by another friend, Harry Evans – this, in my view, is the set for the young English-speaking student of Proust to have: a heavy number, perhaps, to lug to college, but what else do you want with you, *The Lord of the Rings*? – and I made notes all the way. The question loomed, however, of what I was to do with the notes.

I wasn't a Proust expert – I'm still not – so there was no point in writing a learned essay, because it wouldn't be nearly learned enough. I could perhaps write something about the poetry of his prose, but the idea seemed a bit abstruse, and not even he, exotic creature though he had been, was ever interested in alienating the public. On the contrary, he wanted to win prizes, and was quite capable of nobbling a previously hostile critic by taking him to lunch and pretending to consult him. (One of the critics that he nailed by this method, a notorious mediocrity, went on to claim that he had discovered Proust.)

Meanwhile, during this long pondering, the time came when I no longer had to knock myself out in television studios or by flying around the world making documentaries. I was free to do nothing except write critical essays and poems, the two things which I had always thought myself best at, while often wishing that I, like Proust, might have had private means in order to pursue them undisturbed. I had always thought the critical essay and the poem were closely related forms. It was only now, however, that I was struck with the idea of blending the two forms into one, primarily to do my share of recommending a great writer to the next generation, and incidentally to make something out of all those notes I had been taking through half a century of trying to get up to speed with Proust in two different languages.

During that same period, I had been occupied with Dante in the same way, but that made some kind of predictable sense, because I ended up translating him. Proust, however – always needy even when he was alive – demanded something less simple. If I wanted to talk about his poetry beyond the basic level of talking about his language – if I wanted to talk about the poetry of his thought – then the best way to do it might be to write a poem. There is nothing like a poem for transmitting a mental flavour. Instead of trying to describe it, you can evoke it. All it takes is everything you've ever learned about putting words one after the other.

Though I had been ill for several years by the time I got started with the composition of the poem, and had to reconcile myself to the idea that I might not get it done, I was still quite keen not to give my last gasp to a foolish notion. When it comes to the actual, lasting worth of what he is writing, the poet can never assume a sure outcome, but can judge the value of what he has in mind only by how it feels to write it down. That cruel professional fact, however, is just as true at the beginning of one's career as at the end: and one advantage of old age is that one has become used to the uncertain nature of following a hunch, and perhaps less daunted by it.

On that level, I'm bound to say, I felt I was on to something new, strange, and worth the effort. But wouldn't that be the precise feeling I would have if my brains were falling to pieces? It was something I had always wondered about Proust, and nowadays wondered more than ever as my weakened condition approximated his: how could he be sure that his last chapters were really all that great?

Well, they were; and finally, by following his creative instinct all the way until his breath gave out, he gave us something eternally unique. *A la recherche du temps perdu* is a book devoted almost entirely to his gratitude for life, for love, and for art. This much smaller book is devoted to my gratitude for him.

Cambridge, 2016

Gate of Lilacs

1: Origami of the Madeleine

From the taste of the scallop-shell of cake
Made moist by the decoction of lime-blossom
It all unfolds inexorably, the vast
Structure of recollection – in his tongue
L'édifice immense des souvenirs –
Though it's a structure only in the sense
That Gaudi's cathedral in Barcelona
And the weird Watts Towers in Los Angeles –
Eclectic stalagmites of junk – are structures,
Or the sandcastle you helped your daughters build
Before you sat with them to watch the sea
Dismantle it and smooth it out and take it
Back down to where it came from. Architecture
Proust's novel really isn't, though he sets
Great store by the idea of frozen music.
He claims to gaze for hours on end at any
Stone steeple that recalls the gothic spire
Of a Norman church near Balbec. We doubt that,
And then recall Reynaldo Hahn's account
Of how, while touring a strange house, he left
Proust fixed in place, admiring a rose-bush.
When Hahn came back a long time later, Proust
Was still there. Was Proust posing? Hahn asked too,
But eventually concluded he was not,
And so must we. We can regret his wetness –
'My poor, poor little hawthorns!' he would cry,
Clutching them to him as he vowed his grief,
Astounding you that such a total weed
Could ever have become the wise and brave
Soldier for Dreyfus and brought his great book

To full bloom in the hot-house of his dying –
But never doubt his powers of concentration.
When Thomas Mann made notes about how Proust
Made notes, he was acknowledging an equal.
Proust, as Mann saw, was fascinated by
The way a beetle, laying up the food
For the children that would thrive after its death,
Bored through the central nerve of the wrapped body
Of a victim so that, though it could not move,
Still it would live. That was the scrutiny
That Proust could focus on the social life
Of the great world, describing its coherence –
The web that tied the Faubourg to the brothel –
In detailed reverence yet without the curb
Of rigid prejudice against the rise
Of *demos* and its verve. His grandmother
Had shown him the imaginative power
Of tolerance. She thought the local tailor
A true wit and a fine man. Proust took note,
And when the time arrived for him to gauge
The beau monde's actual human sympathy
Behind its poised façade, he had the tools.
Those who believe that nothing really changes
In Proust, that he is just the belle époque
Affirming its longevity, a plush
Box at the opera like Renoir's *La Loge*
In which sits a new face with an old title,
Have it exactly wrong. Everything changes,
And his whole world, the fashionable world,
Is on its way out even as he loves it,
Yielding its primacy to the upcoming
World of creative thought, for which he sets
A standard by including in his scope

The splendour of what was, but is no longer,
Unchallenged. And indeed he was a throwback:
The salons had given way to the cafés –
The new term *demimonde* was coined to cover
A milieu best reported by Colette,
Blessed by the fortune of her humble birth –
The gifted hung out with each other. He,
However, was condemned by privilege
To serve his sentence in a melting prison
Without parole, and see, inside the flow
Of time, what drove it forward yet appeared
To hold it still, with codes of style and manners,
The invitations on the mantelpiece
Lined up like the last guardsmen of an army
That had been routed by Napoleon,
A favour granted and a kiss withheld.
On both the smaller and the greater scale
His texture of perception testifies,
In every paragraph no matter how
Extended, to the pin-point penetration
Of his gaze. He said the literary merit
Of an author could be measured at a glance;
And said it while informing us that Swann
Could instantly assess a smart event
From one peep at the list of attendees.
Swann's snobbery was Proust's, and yet Swann's love
For Odette, which included her bad taste,
Assures us of Proust's seriousness, of how,
Within the limits of his birth, and class,
And poor health, and of being just one person,
He made the whole of life his stamping ground,
Even our jealousies and weaknesses –
A synthesis he introduced by linking

5

The paper flower and the little cake,
All his precision and his subtlety
Flaring to life from a mixed metaphor.

2: The Population of the Velodromes

Years later, that colossal bore Norpois
Recalls that Marcel almost kissed his hand
When he, Norpois, promised to mention him
To Gilberte and Odette. But to remember,
Norpois must first forget. Proust often speaks
About the incalculable proportions
Of recollection and forgetfulness
That make our minds up. Hence the anti-matter
To his matter is included in his book:
Famous for seeing how we bring to mind
The past, he also sees how we do not,
And so he parallels the universe,
Where nebulae as lovely as the jewels
At the throat of the Duchesse de Guermantes
Are balanced by dark blots we know are there
Only because of how they do not shine –
Or so the theory goes, which well might have
The truth of poetry and nothing more,
Like phlogiston, or the globe held up by Atlas.
The past is real but marbled by beliefs
That turned to myth as time eroded them.
Proust sees a great share of the stirring way,
In all this interchange of then and now,
The future forms. Posterity, for him,
Belongs to works of art. A late quartet
Of Beethoven creates its listeners:
Of that, we are the proof. We see advance,
He says, if not the quality of artists,
Then at least the community of minds.
Bergotte, the writer Marcel so admires –

And all the more because the dolt Norpois
Calls him a delinquent mandarin –
Began as the disciple of a speaker
Of brilliance, but who never wrote a word,
And Elstir, though believing painters should
Learn from experience and not example,
Can't talk of Venice, or even about water,
Without the filter of his memories
Of Veronese or Carpaccio.
The individual talent, none the less,
Must underlie the historical group effort.
Artists are made, but first they must be born.
Proust traces talent to its origin
In the awkward age, when almost anything
We do is something we will wish undone
One day, though what we rightly should regret
Is having lost the spontaneity
With which we blundered. In our later lives
We are practical, conforming to the laws
Of good society, but adolescence
Is the only time in which we truly learn.
Three aphorisms in a row, and each
Of the second and the third emerging from
The one before it, deepening the discussion:
The muscle and the sinew of his style
Which carry the fine skin of his assertions
About, say, love: those summaries that sparkle
Even when wrong. Along the esplanade
The little band, the population of
The velodromes, progress as if they were
A human comet. But just one of them
Has eyes of mica. His desire for those
Two discs is proof that it was her whole life

That made him long for her, though in the end –
At the far end of his endless mirror hall –
The eyes, like clocks marked for astronomy
Cut from an opal, of the Princess Nassau,
Arouse a lust for nothing but more time
To catch them with his pen and place them in
His fabric, while untouched by any passion
Beyond the deathless urge to shape the phrase
By which he sends her running to her tomb.

3: The Porcelain Psychologist

In real life, the young Proust sat at the feet
Of Laure Hayman, the demimonde princess
Who educated dukes. His gift to her,
Perhaps presented to her tête-à-tête
In her boudoir, and not at her salon,
Was a fashionable novel bound in silk
From one of her own petticoats. For him,
'My little porcelain psychologist',
She might have put out, but more likely not.
The Marcel in the book is much less given
To the routinely exquisite, as if
The author feared his early reputation
For posturing might stick. Instead he speaks
As the all-wise anatomist of love,
Even when passion's victim. Not a hint
From him of how the little band of girls
Were boys, and how Andrée and Albertine
Were not the girlfriends of the cyclists:
They were cyclists, if only in the sense
That they were strong young men, though not, in fact,
The population of the velodromes.
They were the sons of the high bourgeoisie
And the gentry relaxing in Cabourg
From the rigours of their overprivileged lives.
They were like him, but he was not like them:
His poor health made him frail while they ran free.
Since any object of his young desire
He would imagine rather than approach,
He found it easy to convince himself
That every boy he fell for could have been

A girl, and so on, right throughout his life.
It wasn't vagueness, still less imprecision,
But the feeling, recorded with exactness,
Of being fascinated with the heart's
Potential, of what hadn't happened, quite;
Yet in his mind it had. Agostinelli,
The chauffeur with the long coat and red car,
Who drove him every day through Normandy
At breakneck pace down avenues of poplars,
When otherwise he would have left his bed
On average little more than once a week,
Agostinelli made him an explorer
In every sense, but especially in his thoughts.
They reached back to his boyhood in Cabourg
And gave the driver's thrilling flair and dash
To Albertine in her black jockey-cap.
Thus Albertine, who never did exist,
Though leading him a dance for half the book,
Obsessed him as a spirit he aspired to
Yet made so real that she could break his heart.
By loving others, lying all the time,
She tortures him in every way save one:
He doesn't care that she can't understand
His writings. 'If she had,' he airily
Concludes, as if the point were trivial,
'She would not have inspired them.' Thus the real,
Enriched by the ideal if not, indeed,
Created by it, gains, in Marcel's mind,
Firm outlines from the constant interplay
Of fact and wish. In fact there is no wish
That fails to touch upon our frailties.
We, too, construct a paradise from longings,
Imposing dreams on history. You would swear,

For instance, Proust and Monet were great friends
From how the novel's salon walls seem draped
With pastel images of waterlilies.
Yet Proust and Monet never met. Nor did
We ever meet Proust, though it might seem so
By how he knows our souls when we are faced
With failure to make sense out of the world.
But even he died trying to do that.

4: The Value of the Ruins

In speed, if not in temperature, Proust's book
Is a racing glacier. Though it may linger,
It never languishes, except when Albertine
Takes centuries to prove herself elusive,
As if the author had foreseen his right
Not just to take his time, but to take yours.
But otherwise the prose, far more compressed
Than it might look, is always hard at work
Unpacking trains of thought as they arrive
And valuing the contents of each crate,
Restoring triumph to that wood's-wool word
Excelsior. Nothing goes unexamined,
Not even the traditional gradations
Of the social world to which his keen submission
Was powered by curiosity, as if
Hierarchy were a natural event,
The product of salt water. The dream world
Of the Guermantes cajoles him often to the sea
For images. The women of that clan
Are water nymphs. The Duchesse walks abroad
With the pleasures of the Faubourg Saint-Germain
Contained within her face as if between
The valves, pearl-pale and glossy, of a shell.
But history is catching up with her.
In the era of Madame de Sévigné
Nobody had to know a servant's name,
But Proust can see de Tocqueville's idea –
Equality, even if just imagined –
Was taking hold, simply because the thought
Could now be had. The poor might have a life

Worth living. When the Duc de Saint Simon –
Whom Proust admired, if only for his prose –
Compiled his monumental chronicle
Of court events, nobody in the cast
Existed if their birth had not been high.
Proust wastes no breath regretting the decline
Of what declined because so absolute –
He even leaves the Revolution out –
But in the ruins he still yearns to hear
The smallest detail of the drawing rooms,
Of who wears what and every word they say,
Although he knows – he says so – that true wit
Must falter in the air of the *gratin*,
Where the only function of intelligence
Is lending wings to sheer stupidity.
But he can wait for wit. For now, he needs
The fashionable hostesses, like mothers
Who look all set to kiss him. They do not,
But still they smile on him as he arrives,
And that's enough. The bluestocking hostess –
An aristo in fact, but with pretensions
To nourish the artistically immortal –
Mme de Villeparisis he seeks out
Because she seeks him out, but he knows well
Her fabled politeness adds up to a weapon:
Storing her memories of well-timed grace
She can feel better when the day arrives
Not to invite him. Thus she parodies
The *gratin*, which behaves in the same way,
If with a subtlety it turns to style –
A rondeau of acceptance and rejection
He loathes and fears though all the while he loves it
Because it is on earth, like the rock pool

Which battles with the sea yet guards the life
That teems within it, killing and being killed.
Such self-control he has, to risk his pride
By going where his sensitivities
May well be violated with a glance!
A Jew, although he calls himself a Catholic;
A writer, but no longer the smart boy
He once was, with his epigrams and squibs
And parodies kept short to be amusing
But not for too long; and a pederast,
Though quiet with it. His appeal to those
Whose invitations line his mantelpiece
Comes to depend on what he knows of them:
Since nothing interests them except themselves
The fact that he can put each name in place
In the celestial map of their existence
Confirms to them their realized ideal.

5: The Red Plush Bench

For all the upper crust are idealists
When it comes to their position. Young Gilberte,
Who played once in the gardens of the Champs
Élysées while Marcel went mad for her,
In old age turns into a raging snob
Because she has become herself at last:
A play-time princess once, a real one now,
Or, if you like, a fake one now, and real
No longer, having switched joy for hauteur.
Saint-Loup, in the same way, but with more brains –
It is the intellectual in Marcel
That he admires and gives his friendship to –
Always remains, even when he rebels,
Assured in his high rank. In fact he strives
To show his mistress, Rachel the *cocotte*,
That the world, because revolving around him,
Revolves around her too. He showers her
With gifts proclaiming, not so much her worth,
As his, a profligate expenditure
Which leads Proust to conclude that his dear friend,
Who could have had his girl for twenty francs,
Spends millions all to serve his ideal self.
But Saint-Loup's ideal self is what Proust loves:
The unplanned gestures of his vivid life,
The way he makes a gangway of the shelf
Head-high behind the crowded red plush bench
In the *grande salle* that swirls with light-filled smoke,
And runs without a stumble, held aloft
By nothing but his magic confidence.
For Proust, whose awkward hours in uniform

Remained a joke, Saint-Loup's athletic skill –
His fitness for the memorable gesture –
Was one more angle of a dream come true,
A moment when assurance was embodied,
Not just personified. Proust loved Saint-Loup,
Although, in life, he had to make him up,
Assembling him from several high-born models
With names a block long, but the low-born one,
And the one who counted when it came to zest,
Was probably Cocteau, whose stylish gifts –
His diamond passport to a lifetime's fame –
Were similarly seldom far removed
From an exclusive context. In the end,
However, at the Tour d'Argent receptions,
The audience of influential people
Reverently hanging on his every quip
Included the Gestapo, who played host.
He killed them, but in quite a different sense
They would have killed Proust. Cocteau got all that,
But couldn't quell his urge to shine: a flaw
Proust would have understood, indeed foretold,
Knowing he had that fault within himself.
But he knew where it was, and why the artist
Can't flirt with power. He must break with it,
And, if the well-connected world conceives
A taste for cruelty, kiss it goodbye.

6: Toulouse-Lautrec's Striped Drinks

Proust calls Charlus the soul of indiscretion:
A recognition that the Baron's knack
For scandal is a cornucopia
Of gifts for any novelist. In life,
Le Comte Robert de Montesquiou, a model,
If not the only model, for Charlus,
Was what Proust might have been, a minor writer
Of precious things, though Montesquiou, who had
No qualms about his own proclivities,
Would doubtless have conceived the urge to bind
A book of his slight writings in the cloth
Of some boy's underpants. Yet Proust would not
Have been so at his ease. The portrait by
Boldini is a stunner. Montesquiou
Is dressed to kill. Regard the grey kid gloves,
The points of his moustache like daggers raised
Against the march of the ill-bred. A shame
That he was never caught in his white suit
By Whistler, though the portrait in the Frick
Of Montesquiou in evening dress is held
By some to outclass even the Boldini
For sheer cool, the Bad Baron at his height
Of glamour. Still, the way that he appears –
The angle of his cane, that black foulard –
Today in the Musée d'Orsay, suffices
To show us why Proust ate the concept up
Of dandyism as a form of art,
And, later, spat it out. The exquisite,
In Proust's eyes, was a realm designed for women,
And Charlus in decay, mascara smeared,

Tells us that being gay was not, for Proust,
A way of life, but just a part of life,
And any monomania would be punished
By a withering within. Thus, on the heights,
Where those whose greatest aim is to hobnob
With one another and keep others out,
The anti-Dreyfusards have sacrificed
Their main advantage – to have no ideas –
And where they once could revel in the freedom
Of judging everything by style alone –
Essentially, to do so *was* their style –
Now they are hampered by a theory
Of Jewish sabotage. But Proust, although
No saboteur – he loved the ormolu
And mirrors with gilt frames a mile too much
To seek a refuge in bohemia,
Though that's precisely where he's ended up,
Along with us – can see a compensation:
The way is opening for a new elite
Of those who incarnate the liberal mind,
Discovering itself because the force
Of obscurantism has energized
What once was just a lazy prejudice
And turned its somnolence to a crusade,
Shrinking what was a wide, if witless, view
Into the eye-slit of a rusting visor.
Saint-Loup breaks up with Rachel. He will not
Forget her. She retains her influence
In his life, but her independent nature
Asserts itself as once it never could
When choked by necklaces that cost the earth.
She moves on, and becomes, after the war –
The war in which Saint-Loup, alas, is killed –

A famous actress, hailed in the salons
For her artistic stature, and not only
For being the close friend of the Duchesse
De Guermantes. And yet Rachel, in her splendour,
Is still for Dreyfus, as she's always been.
The Faubourg and the brothel meet each other:
Perhaps like oil and water, but within
The same tall shining tumblers, to evoke
The drinks served by Lautrec at his soirées,
A knickerbocker-glory dynamite
With coloured layers. Swirling in the liquid,
Intelligence and sensitivity
Like interloping streaks of cloud are trails
Of storms sent to disturb a world. A war,
A war between the wars, is happening
Throughout Proust's book, though all he tells us of
The Western Front is how the sky was lit
At night with flares and shellfire streaming up,
Drawn by the Gothas and the Zeppelins:
The bursts of colour in the neutral stars,
Bright tokens of what Paris had been spared
Because the vandal armies never came.

7: An Edifice Subverted

But the other war, the battle for the soul
Of France, scars every page. The social world,
Made more hierarchical than ever
By the democratic upsurge, has the gloss
Proust loves, yet it has set its teeth against
The intellect that he admires. His task
Must be to bring two forces into balance
By how he writes, and find the power to do so
In the hissing sparks they shower when they clash.
In real life, Proust would dine with anti-Semites –
Léon Daudet, the brother of Alphonse,
Who wrote that perfect little novel *Sappho*,
Was only one of them – but was not shocked
To see them stand revealed when the bell rang
As anti-Dreyfusards. For after all,
They were only authors. But when, on the page,
He made Charlus say nobody could be
A Jew and French too, that was a real fear:
Fear of a stupid notion soaking upwards
Into the edifice Proust once had thought
Thought-proof, and therefore safely occupied
With niceties of pomp and precedence.
He says of the Duchesse that when she talked
To him about the Faubourg Saint-Germain
She furnished him with literature, but when
She talked of literature she sounded like
The product of her class. Looming before him
Was the prospect of his much-loved ambience
Not yet sclerotic, not yet cancer-ridden,
But faltering as it threatened its own heart

By taking its long-cherished bigotries
For principles, and playing politics.
Proust knew that you can play at anything,
But not at being serious. Hence his style,
Born out of thinking to give thought a voice,
Returns always from any rhapsody
To frame a law. Of love, he says, we can
Speak and behave in philosophical
Detachment only when we are not in it.
Alas, it's largely true, and if we don't
Entirely believe it, still we'd better
Accept that it might not be always false,
Or else condemn ourselves to a dream world,
When the real world is a battlefield. Proust might
Be Darwin when he writes of nature. His
Admiring critic Jean-François Revel
Called the book's plenitude of nature scenes
A showcase for nocturnal butterflies,
But they are crucial to the mental texture –
They are the hard truth our humanity
Emerges from, and should recall, if only
To see why we must live by better rules.

8: Excursus on Prose Style

At the Grand Hotel in Balbec, on the terrace –
The gulls float like white petals on the sea –
The dowager Mme de Cambremer,
Tempting Marcel to luncheon at Féterne,
Where she plays the great lady, waves at him
The promise he will 'find' among her guests
The Comte de Crisenoy. Marcel remarks,
But silently, that he had never lost him
For the simple reason he had never met him.
He is cruel to her, but only in his thoughts,
And thus not cruel at all compared with what
The great do to the less great with their snubs
And polished sneers. For Proust has merely noted
A point of language. But the point lays bare
Her passion, almost desperate, to maintain
Her rank, though exiled far from the Faubourg,
Put out to grass here at the edge of things,
Where, just beyond the edge, the glittering sea
Echoes the drawing rooms now lost to her.
Oceans of trinkets and a velvet cape,
A hat perched perilously on her wig,
Her strained get-up is not the give-away:
Like her toothbrush moustache, it's just a quirk.
Proust's registration of the way she looks
Would, on its own, be no more than a spoof.
It's what she says, in just a single phrase –
Or, if you like, it's what he makes her say –
That proves him the anatomist. His prose
Is a descriptive catalogue of all
The things of this world in one gallery.

The painters that he loved, we should remember,
Had clean outlines. In that brave photograph
Of 1921, only a year
Before his death – the photograph in which
He stands so straight and seems to have a chest,
Though it was padding, packed beneath his shirt
To save him from the air – look to his right
And you will see the Jeu de Paume. He'd come,
For the last time he would ever leave his room,
To see the exhibition of Vermeer
(Before whose *View of Delft* he makes Bergotte
Fall ill and die), the master of lit space,
Whose clarities and textures are like his,
Clean-cut and accurate. Never believe
That Proust is merely an Impressionist
(The Impressionists aren't 'merely' anyway)
Breathing a soft and pastel atmosphere
That blurs the furniture and takes the edge
Off any fleshly curve the way Vuillard,
In all his concentrated prettiness,
Makes any female's face soft as the clothes
She wears and as the sofa she sits down in:
The chintz which in real life is glazed and hard,
But his paint turns it into brushed cashmere.
Proust strays, but not to hide. He sees the sense
Of form that underlies the fields of colour
Of the Impressionists. His sentences
Grow lengthy when he speculates and ponders,
But start and end in just the brevity
French aphorists have been so famous for
Since Pascal concentrated and distilled
The essence of Montaigne. La Rochefoucald
And Vauvenargues were models for Chamfort,

Who, when the Revolution threatened him
With a second stretch in the Madelonnettes
(The rats were heralds of the guillotine),
Attempted to forestall his execution
With a pistol and a knife, and got it wrong,
And, even as he lay there bathed in blood,
Fashioned with care a fitting epigram:
If not for me, that might have gone quite well.
(I've just remembered La Bruyère, who said
That self-indulgence and severity
Towards others were the same vice. He was right:
A quite rare quality among the wits.)
That whole tradition of terse cracking wise
Is there in Proust's prose, leavened by respect
For actuality, the neutral gaze
Of the Encyclopedia: a mix of thought
With brutal fact, like bird-shot with bird-seed,
Art with the artless: the art of Diderot,
So broke at one stage that he sold his books
To Catherine the Great. (She left them there
In Paris, with a payment so he might
Look after them, although she must have known
His prose was gunpowder in quiet form.)
Back in the business of philosophy,
He found time to compose such master works
As his chapter on the woman blind from birth
Whose sense of hearing attained such a pitch
That she could see with it. Such treasure troves
Of observation wed to poetry
Were there for Proust to bend to a new use:
The work of fiction that flows like the facts
Of life, an ocean going through your hands
Into the future, and whose movement is

The actual subject, which is hard to grasp
Only because the instant is. But what
Combines these symbiotic elements –
The burning moment and the grand expanse –
Into a compound can be overlooked
Merely because it marked the fluent style
Of Proust's dead enemy, Sainte-Beuve, whose sin,
In Proust's eyes, was his urge to tangle up
The artist with the art, thus to locate
The way that writers wrote in how they lived.

9: The Rhythm of Inclusion

For Proust, who guessed a long way in advance
That he would scarcely live at all, this view –
A view which, logically pursued, confines
All works of art to being reproductions
Of the individuals who give rise to them –
Was worse than a cliché, it was a crime.
And so he aimed a whole book at Sainte-Beuve
(As a great chef might construct a custard pie
Specifically to fit a certain face),
But, studying his subject, could not help
Catching the rhythm of his bête noire's voice,
And thus, in all the purlieus of Proust's book
Where you expect but do not find Balzac –
We hear his name but no hint of his keen
Interest in income and expenditure –
You find the cadence of a bourgeois critic
Who dined at Magny's with the Goncourt brothers
In comfort, well content with his prestige.
By echoing, against his will, the prolix
Outpouring of a comprehensive view –
The Monday articles by which Sainte-Beuve
Entranced a nation – Proust entranced the world,
And still does, more than ever, now the world
Disintegrates into a trillion signs
That no machine makes sense of on its own,
Except by breaking up the paragraphs,
Making italics roman, and in general
Packaging literature to suit the Web.
Sainte-Beuve, who would have found him second-rate
Like any first-rate artist except one

(Sainte-Beuve praised Victor Hugo, though perhaps
From guilt for his affair with Hugo's wife),
Thus helped to give us Proust, by bringing prose
To levels where it took a genius
To take it further. Not that Proust acknowledged
A debt to either of the French traditions,
Whether the quick barb or the easy sweep:
He wanted to be Ruskin, whom he read
As haltingly as most of us read French.
It doesn't matter. Proust incorporates:
The second thing his prose does, but the first
Is having so much to include, and here
It is his range that dazzles us so much
We can hardly see for looking. Even when
Marcel's deep love for the Duchesse has faded
Into a friendship where he is no longer
Blind to her faults – her hypocritical
Indifference to her servants is enough,
In his eyes, to demolish her position
As an angel – still her stylish qualities
Obsess him. Waiting for her carriage home
From an evening *chez* the Princesse de Guermantes,
She stands poised at the head of the front steps
In her cloak like something from Tiepolo,
Her rubies brilliant at her throat. But then
She skips across the steps to give her blessing
To Mme de Gallardon, whom she shut out
From her acquaintance but has now forgiven –
The grand forgive a victim for the crime
That they themselves committed – and recalls,
In how she moves, the lightness and the grace
Proust gave Saint-Loup high up on the banquette.
Proust doesn't spell it out, but the two scenes

Mimic each other in their pace and diction,
And besides, the airy charm is in the blood:
Saint-Loup is also a Guermantes. They are
A blood-line that gives style to influence,
Though in the course of Proust's long narrative
(For once a word is fitting that should never,
Ever be used except about the arts)
Their power shows a hint of growing weak,
As if, in France, the shock-wave of the Commune
Had shifted even the grandest families
Further towards the edge of history
Where royalty had long preceded them
To darkness from the sharp-edged precipice.
For Proust, however, nothing beats the Duchesse
As an arbiter of all that's elegant:
Just as, in life, the woman she was based on,
Elisabeth, Comtesse Greffulhe, held sway
In the beau monde by her sure taste for beauty
As much as her position, which she risked
By leading the descent from the Faubourg
To see the *Ballets Russes*, almost as if
The great were in attendance on the artists,
And not the other way about. For Proust,
The fashionable world is a theatre,
And this theatre is a reef. It teems
With life, and he not only names the names
Of the grandees, but of the servants. Françoise,
A servant in his family since his birth,
Has 'simple but unerring taste' in clothes,
Which tells you, at a blow, that Proust thought style
A thing of talent, not just privilege.
So there was nothing that he did not see
Or hear, but was he deaf and blind to love?

Surely the biggest subject of his book
Is passion, and our biggest question for him
Is whether he was right about that too.

10: Adventures of the Aerosol Elixir

Touchstone and lodestone, lynchpin, holy scroll
Of the learned industry based on his name,
The Quest for Proust should not start with his book:
It ends there. What he really felt, or knew,
Was never crystallized before he wrote,
But came true in the writing. The effect
Of all encyclopedists is to make us
Punish ourselves that they can know all that.
They never did. Before they wrote it down
They had not yet become themselves in full,
And while they studied hard and long, they changed
And grew, and so with Proust, whose every theme
Is brought to being in his masterpiece,
Not brought to it. The same way molten rock
Makes possible the earth on which we walk,
The way he writes about desire reminds us
Of what it was when we were still too young
To know about its power, but everywhere
We felt it, and in everything. The world
Was soaked in it. The sensual, Proust insists,
When it strikes us in the hot part of the year,
Is less a longing for a girl's cool kiss
Than a thirst for orangeade. The areas
Of lust that he knows best are nearly all
Pre-sexual, or at any rate pre-conscious
Of what sex is. Thus he is at his most
Precise about the generalized. When, later,
The sexual world splits up into its genders
He prides himself on how he can record
Behaviour, see how sex determines action;

But the act itself is often non-specific,
A thing of hints for all its urgency.
Even the rhapsody on deviance
That forms Part One of *Sodom and Gomorrah*
Is chastened by its references to flowers,
As if the author's mind were swamped by blooms
And lust could have the softness of a petal.
Marcel sees Charlus in the flagrant act
Of getting whipped, but of his basic tastes
Nothing is said. Not one male mouth is kissed,
So what goes on? And Françoise saw Marcel
In bed with Albertine, but what did they,
Exactly, do? And Albertine likes girls;
Her means of progress is to swing both ways.
All set to flee even when standing still,
Her essence is to be ambiguous,
And those of the book's people who are not
Could well, we feel, become so overnight,
Until you don't know where you are. Can it
Be real that Saint-Loup ends up turning gay,
Or isn't that a case of the tenacious
Belief of some gay intellectual men
That all men are bisexual underneath
And masculinity is just a pose?
If that were so, then he was fooling Rachel
For all that time. It just seems one too many
Unlikely thing to hear about Saint-Loup,
Always supposing that we lend our credence
To the scenes in which his fellow officers
Approve his war-like stature in the barracks
Yet never notice that around his neck
He wears Marcel like a wet feather boa.
Unlikelihood, however, is trumped always

By what Marcel can see. Somehow he guesses
Charlus, when vamping Madame de Surgis
(The plaything of the Duke, a liaison
Put up with by his wife, if not endorsed),
Has aims of getting closer to her sons.
Saint-Loup, however, doesn't spot the ploy,
Believing that his uncle feels desire
Only for women. Later, he learns better,
Or worse, if we believe that an illusion
Can better serve a civilized existence.
From time to time, we all do, but not Proust,
Who tells the truth like one marked out for death,
The only real distortion in his story
Imposed by one fact: he was always dying.

11: The Copy of a Kiss

The naturalist who makes gay sex a garden
Is heaping hills of flowers around a coffin,
And it is his. Right from the start, his book
Is ending in a transubstantiation
By which the genders blend with one another
Into a *Liebestod*, and to the end
It is beginning in his love of women,
So Albertine, when caught out in her vice –
Marcel finds out she had a three-way fling
With Madame de Vinteuil and her friend –
Still tastes to him the way his mother tasted
When she came to the nursery to kiss him.
Late in the book he takes a page to say
His memory kept no copy of the kiss
With which he first acquired from Albertine
His knowledge of how ecstasy could feel,
But early in the book, when they blend mouths,
He tells us how the angle of their noses
Had mutually to be agreed so as
To maximize the contact. Every pore
Of her young skin is in the picture. Breath
From her lungs sends its perfume into his.
Saintsbury once said the flavour of a lyric
Is like a smiling girl. So it is here:
The feminine invents the sensual
In our erotic childhood, and then
Imperiously unfolds to fill the mind.
(When I was first in love, on holiday
With my mother at Katoomba, New South Wales,
The little girl – we called her Lacy Skirts –

Would dodge my doting gaze down corridors
And swerve into the garden with a flourish
Of her white frock, and now all I remember
Is how she frowned, and how I lay awake
Planning the speeches that would make her smile:
The lovelorn hunger I still write with now
Was born then, so whenever I read of Swann
Wasting his life with longing for Odette
Even when she was his, I see myself
Back there in the Blue Mountains, yet again
Consumed by the sweet torments of a love
That never happened, unless this is it.)
Like the Fortuny gowns Elstir admires
Because they bring back the Venetian light
Of classic painters, Proust's book is a swathe
Of pleats that open swirling into space
As a woman pirouettes, wrapped in a wave
Of cloth that follows her, still chasing her
When it has caught her. Just the way it moves
Is feminine in essence. So is he:
Perhaps we all are. During his time in Venice
In 1900, Proust fell for a bar-girl,
Or might have. She is in *The Sweet Cheat Gone*,
Where the Venice flashback is almost a novel
In itself, as Marcel informs us firmly
His love for Albertine is dead and buried:
Done with. Forgotten. A closed book. So over.
Is he the one he's striving to convince?
And was the pretty girl a pretty boy
Who waited on him at the Florian?
Proust must have known, but Marcel doesn't say.
All this, however, counts as a flash forward,
For first the girl must tease him towards God

As Beatrice did to Dante. In his mind
He had the amorous vision, even if
His body, as it were, thought otherwise.
'As Aristotle tells us in the second
Chapter of . . .' So pipes M. Pierre,
Historian of the Fronde, but no one pays
Him any heed except, of course, for Proust,
Anatomist of bores. But almost every
Man he invents is boring. The great Duke –
The walking castle of the clan Guermantes –
Writes novels about life in the *gratin*
That are worthy of his grocer. What he does
Is hardly worth recounting. What he is
Is all that matters, and what matters most
Is the poem he is married to. And she,
The stately, subtle and divine Duchesse,
Can be as coldly nasty as her husband,
Though she never, unlike him, joins in the cry
Against Dreyfus, which would undoubtedly
Have put Proust off: at least we trust it would.
A royal couple fabulously dressed
And heading for a ball, the pair are told
That their close friend is dying. They blame him
For selfish timing. Marcel is appalled,
But all the more he must admire her style,
For this is the perennial human struggle,
Not politics. Thus she keeps to her role,
Which is to fascinate him. He loves her
Past anything he felt for Albertine,
For that was merely passion's fleeting madness,
And Oriane de Guermantes is the face –
As poised as the ephemeral held still –
Of death, as nowadays some film star is

The face of Dior, of Saint Laurent, Chanel
Or Givenchy, and what we see in Proust
Is how the genius prepares to take
His place in history even while he lives
His life as someone who knows very well
How beauty can be false. But falsity
Is in life too, and ruthless. Think of all
Those plain companions back there in our youth
We should have liked, but just pretended to,
And never saw again. The Duchesse smiles.
She makes her way to us. She knows our name,
And all our childish passions come to this.

12: Gardens of the Artists

Or would do, if we had no home to go to,
No wife and family. That fitted Proust,
Whose gift for populated loneliness
Had left him free, after his mother died,
To seek adventure. Though he scarcely moved –
In his book, Paris is the only city,
With Venice treated as a kind of suburb
Plus extra water and a quick side trip
To Padua, to check out the Giottos –
His mind was everywhere, assessing threads
Of quality and squalor that passed through
The upper layers of society
On their journey into space. The Verdurins
Play host to Ski, the Polish sculptor. Ski
Is a footloose exiled arts type who can do
A bit of everything and make it look
As if he isn't even on the make.
What gets Marcel, though, isn't his brass front
But the way his clambering mediocrity
Brings out the philistine pretentiousness
Of Mme Verdurin. She places him
Above Elstir for talent, because Ski,
Although his indolence befits his gift,
Knows no restrictions. 'Ski paints anything
You ask: on cuff-links, lintels . . .' There she stands,
Skewered in all her pomp, and far more sad
Than when she turns up in the Venice scene
Much later, far too old, a frump. One day,
And that day oddly soon, it seems, she will
Become the Duchesse de Guermantes. Yes, time

Gets warped by Proust, but when things don't add up –
Some personage turns old and doddering
With dazzling promptitude, or else another
Shows up for the big party at the end
In strangely good shape for someone who must
Have been worm food for fifteen years at least –
It's best to let them go, and concentrate
On how he handles the true calculus
Of character. Children he just can't do:
It's lucky no one has them. Any child
We meet in the vast layout of his pages
Is on its way to adulthood already,
And, when in Paris, neatly disappears,
Leaving the cast a free hand to wreak havoc
On one another's love lives. That aside,
The social paradise Marcel inhabits
Is hyper-realistically shot through
With rancour and venality. Morel,
The lover of Charlus, has stature as
A violinist. Low birth reasserts
Its cheap grip, and by bribing the chauffeur
To hike the mileage he can take a cut
From the money Charlus pays out without looking.
Later we hear how Morel, as a soldier
Fights bravely at the front, but when he serves
As the Baron's toy-boy, he exacts the price
By forcing his mean master to largesse.
Noblesse oblige, but the noble ends up cheated,
Cheated by love. In the self-consuming frenzy
That Proust believes to be love's only form,
Frankness, he says, is quite impossible
Between the lovers, even about the past.
As their love deepens, they pretend they never

Said what they said beforehand, in the freedom
Of speech that should be part of their enjoyment,
But now can't be. And yet by getting lost
In burning love's miasma of bad faith
The imagination opens, as Bergotte,
Proust says, was educated by his women.
The same was true, we gather, of Elstir,
Who rose like Neptune through a sea of models,
And one of them, let's try not to forget,
Was young Odette in her first days of hooking,
Before she bent herself to the long task
Of driving Swann out of his well-heeled mind.
The greatest aphorism in a book
Of aphorisms surely is, some think,
The one about how nothing is as precious,
In our possession of a certain woman,
As what she teaches us about ourselves
By causing us to suffer. Crackling stuff,
But scarcely Montesquieu (I mean the sage,
Not the exquisite toff), and anyway
Proust's fragments, though they seem, sometimes, to claim
An independent life, have something else
In mind, a vast coherence like the sea,
The sea before the days of plastic bottles,
The sea that took down junk as if it were
The rain. In this, his special fortitude
Is to accept that all he most adores
In life – even the arts, even the souls
(Those gardens where no salon rules apply)
Of Elstir and Bergotte – is powered by
A maelstrom of desire, and might return
To tumult unless regulated by
The intellect, which is itself a passion.

13: You Saw Nothing in Hiroshima

From that viewpoint, his book has no sound-bites
To take away, or even a summation:
It merely has a tone, as when he says
It's not because those we have known are dead
That our affection for them fades, it is
Because we, too, are dying. But he might
Be fooling us. 'One lies all one's life long':
He said that, too. His book, big for a book,
Is still small for a world. Alain Resnais
Made films that echoed him but we won't find
In Proust the harbingers of Delphine Seyrig
Draped on an enigmatic balustrade
In Marienbad while the men in black ties play
The match game, or the desolate voice-over
Of *Hiroshima Mon Amour*. Those things –
At least as consciously aestheticized
As almost anything dreamed up by Proust –
Were done strictly for us. If he had lived
To watch the Prussian aristocracy,
Having regained its honour in the plot
Of July 20th, 1944,
Retire from politics but lend its means
To service – had he seen the Gräfin Dönhoff,
A true-blue *grande dame* to the castle born,
Give all her taste and judgement and prestige
To her newspaper *Die Zeit* and so help guide
Her nation back to take its leading role
In a democratic Europe – Proust might well
Have noted that his picture of a class
Losing its vestiges of relevance

Was slightly overdrawn. To punish him
For incompleteness, though, is to be Xerxes
Beating the sea with rods. Not even he
Could see the times to come. Best to give thanks
For the patience Stefan Zweig ascribed to Rilke,
Which Proust shared: he could wait for the return
Of memories in his blood. No doubt we could
Leave him unread. A friend of mine who speaks
French perfectly, knows Flaubert note for note,
And goes on French TV to talk about
France vis-à-vis Great Britain and vice versa,
Still hasn't read a word of Proust, and that,
For him, is best. My daughters both revisit
All of Jane Austen every year or two,
And neither feels the need for information
About a bunch of snobs across the Channel:
They'd rather binge-watch *The West Wing* again,
A perfect pleasure the whole family shares.
I see their point, but speaking for myself,
Proust's book gave me the courage to admit –
As did the culture of Japan, as did
The architecture of the Winter Palace,
The glass and plaster of the Amalienburg
And many fine and delicate things throughout
Our heritage – think of the Graces swaying
In Botticelli's *Primavera*, think
Of the bronzes that a scuba diver found
Two hundred metres down in the sand floor
Of the sea at Capo Riace in our time,
Those bronzes that had spent two thousand years
Being beautiful down there – think of all that
And too much more that I have no time now
Even to name, now that my death comes close –

To admit that almost all I've ever loved
Exists in contrast to my nature. I,
A clumsy man, and thoughtless, with small gifts
Of subtlety or intuition, have
No natural business fondling the fine-drawn
And exquisite. Tanagra figurines,
If given to my keeping, I'd have used
For paperweights. We're talking a born vandal,
A Goth dyed in the wool. Yet all my life
People and things I've loved have always shared
Unnecessary grace. Life would have worked
As well without it, so the preference felt
Like selfishness, the ripping of fine things
From conquered walls in envious revenge,
Though really human life produced refinement
Before society was even thought of:
When people still were hunting what they ate
And eating it without a single napkin,
Some of them painted, deep inside their caves,
Pictures of animals at least as pure
And sure as any by Picasso, who
Already, in another part of Paris,
Had plundered all of history for his palette
While Proust still lived. Proust sanctions such excess
By tracing our concern with how things look
Not just back to the urge to reproduce –
How can we separate the sighing wish
To touch the owner of a pretty face
From the poised and learned way that we prefer
The light and airy *Virgin of the Rocks*
In the Louvre to the steely one in London? –
But further back than that, to where and when
The nautilus, adrift on the long swell,

Was intricate and lovely and no one
Was even there to see it. Art came first:
We just gave it a name. It is the task
Of Proust to fix in place the flux of things –
The stream that Heraclitus said is never
The same each time that we step into it –
For long enough to tell us why its taste
Takes so much bitterness to make it sweet.

14: We'll Always Have Paris

Proust left behind him a great lie more deadly
Than any hatched by Albertine. He said
That love consumes itself in jealousy
And can't survive a marriage. How could he
Know such a thing? A passion is just nature,
And nature boasts at least one butterfly
That plants a stink-bomb in the female after
Having his way with her, so that no other
Male butterfly will want her. There are human
Societies like that, but we try hard
To keep their males from marrying our daughters.
A marriage is what civilization makes
Out of an urgency. Proust saw all that
But placed no value on the battle damage –
The fraying patience, even with the best
Will in the world, and, when there is the worst,
The betrayals, the retreats from the betrayals;
The nagging thought that you have been held back,
And, even more corrosive, that you have
Held back the one whose life is joined to yours;
The living hell of seeing your child sicken,
As Proust himself was sick, but this is worse,
Because there will be nothing left but loss –
All these and all the other disappointments
(They haunt even your moments of shared laughter
At your sheer luck in having found someone
Better than you to help you find where passion
Is meant to lead beyond delirium)
That come after the love-storm and before
The soul lies down to sleep. And it's from those,

Of course, that we become wise, if we do:
Which makes a nonsense of Proust's fine idea
That early youth is when we learn what matters.
The opposite, it could be said, applies:
Only the married learn a thing. Proust never
Found any of that out except by dint
Of observation, never quite the same
As going through the mill. He didn't have to:
He had his marvellous book to write. His freedom
From all ties makes him childish: and yet what
A child. To wish him different would be like
The wish for a nice Wagner. Proust is worth
A mass, like Paris. At the end of *Casablanca*
Bogart and Ingrid Bergman part forever
With the motto that rings bells still in young hearts:
We'll always have Paris. And so we do:
But the city is intact by chance. If Proust
Could rise for just a day from Père Lachaise
And walk awhile he would see little different
Apart from that dull shaft on Montparnasse
(Let's not forget, though, that the Eiffel Tower
Was brand new in his time, as was the church
Of Sacré Coeur perched mosque-like on Montmartre:
It's just that they both happened to look good)
But he would soon hear that the *Wehrmacht* marched
Triumphant down the Champs-Élysées and
The Jews left from the Drancy velodrome
For the journey east to death. Paris survived,
But might, had Hitler settled in to govern,
Have echoed what occurred in Petersburg
After the revolution, when the high life
Of title, taste and patronage was exiled
Or just wiped out. Catastrophes like that,

As well as all the millions that they kill,
Derail the history even of the arts:
Who now remembers the Troubetzkoy sculptures
(He had a way of making metal look
As crisp as biscuit that left Rodin seeming
Almost ham-fisted by comparison)
Of those princesses and grand duchesses
Or just plain duchesses and bankers' wives,
Or the pastel portrait by Pasternak's father
Of a Jewess of the high-born bourgeoisie?
Eliminated like class enemies,
Even as images proscribed for decades,
They dropped from our regard. In Stalin's fiefdom –
I speak as a Kerenskyite, a Kulak,
A Wrecker and a Social Fascist who,
From hopeless passion for Akhmatova,
Might just have stuck around to be wiped out –
It was Year Zero always. The belle époque
Of Russia came to Paris. Diaghilev
Was Proust in all but name. The Little Phrase
Of Vinteuil teasing us throughout the novel –
It's there and there again like all those drawings
By Watteau studying the different ways
A woman's smile could look: drawings that Proust
Admired, thrilled by the science of an artist –
Undoubtedly pays tribute to Saint-Saëns,
But echoes also, surely, that sublime
Descending cadence signalling the end
Of *Petroushka*, and I think always of how
Mass murder sent its ripples to New York
And gave us Balanchine: a tragic gain.
Cultures can die, or flee. Proust knew that well.
Behind the shimmer, harsh truths rule his book.

Here is no fantasist. His poetry
Begins in prose, and we should not allow
An ignorance of French to keep us from him,
For he is more than style: or say it this way,
His style is more than his own language. Start
With Scott Moncrieff's translation, which well might
Arouse an ache to make a start on French
(It isn't that hard, once you realize
That it's impossible. *Courage, mes braves!*)
But will enrich you even if you don't
Get enough French to travel on the Metro,
Saying without a blush the lovely name
Of the Gate of Lilacs. Poetry: and yet
The way Proust thinks has music of its own
More beautiful than anything inherent
In his native tongue – for in that, after all,
Sade and Céline wrote too – and in the spell
Of Proust's great paragraphs we hear and see
The ocean into which we all, as he did,
Must sink back, our achievements left behind –
Whether a necessary task fulfilled
Or else whole symphonies – and be reclaimed
By nature, which has no mind of its own
But simply makes us welcome, as the ashes
Of Maria Callas, spread on the Aegean,
Were first a cloud, and then a mist, then nothing
But an everlasting song reduced to atoms
Which, though they drift apart, are still together
In the memories of those of us who live.

15: I'll drown my books

Until we die. Too late to rule that out,
And as I write there's nothing but the drugs
To keep me going. I'll call that a break:
My family guards me from the world, which should
Expect no more from me. This secret book
I needn't even finish. Proust got caught
By time, his special subject, long before
He finalized his manuscript, which he just
Pretended he had sorted out, and heartbreak
Had caught him before that. Agostinelli
Turned pilot when the war came. At Antibes
He crashed into the Bay of Angels. Proust,
As his protective callousness attests –
He says the only function of the face
Of his now truly vanished Albertine
Had been to remind him of the dawn –
Must surely have not thought he would outlive
His beautiful young man. But grief is there
Throughout his magnum opus. He was like that,
And so am I. Perhaps there lies the reason
For my love of his writing. From my start
In Sydney far away, I longed for Paris.
Those tipped-in colour plates in Skira books
About Degas, Lautrec, Manet, Seurat –
They came as proof that in the post-war world
The means to privilege might reach anyone –
Consoled me for the stroke of fate that tore
My father from my mother and left me,
For all my energy and glowing health,
A head-case hungry for a context. But

In those days Paris was intransigent –
Cops checked your papers as if you had come
To kill De Gaulle, and only a rich Yank
Could think of being a poor student there –
So I was poor in London. Later on,
In Cambridge, I picked up the Livres de Poche
Proust set, and I began the endless task
Of learning French from it. For fifteen years
I stumbled through it. Other writers go
Crazy for Henry James, who praised, in Browning,
The 'slanting coloured lights'. But Proust had more
Of those, in my view, and without conveying
The same sense that a craze for subtlety
Had taken leave of substance. No, for me
Proust was the man, that droopy, wheezing dweeb:
Although I must say that in evening dress
As captured deftly by Jacques-Emile Blanche
In 1895, he looked much better
Than I ever did at Glyndebourne. By the end,
However, time had turned into a wreck
A body that was never strong. He lay
As powerless as the child that he had been
When waiting an eternity for his mother
To climb the stairs and kiss him. Now my turn
Has come to quit the stage, I only hope
I've used my time between strength and departure,
The extra time, a tenth as well as he.
Ah, soldier: what you did. It's in those shelves
Of books by and about you I will leave
Here in my kitchen which has no cork walls,
Only the English early summer light
That pours in from the garden where my wife
And I meet on my balcony to count

The birds and wonder how to make them stay.
We've overdone the food, I think. Next spring,
If I'm still here to help, we might dial down
The chow supply. It's like Maxim's out there.
It's too much. Proust is sometimes that as well,
But not so often as he is austere,
Saying enough to make you see the rest,
As the face of Oriane is not described
But only conjured from your memories
Of everything that you have loved. And soon
All that I love will leave me, as I go
First into silence, then the fire, and then
The harbour water, in which there will be
At last no room to breathe, no time to think:
No time to think even of you, Marcel.

Postscript

Proust was a very clever man, and had nothing to do with his day except observe, study and write. His powers of observation were as acute as Dante's, Shakespeare's or Goethe's, but we might say the same of Lucretius, or of Homer when he registered in a set of syllables the quivering of a bowstring: when Conrad said that the writer's aim was 'above all, to make you see', he forgot to say that the ability to observe is the writer's first qualification. But we ought to think harder about Proust's capacity for study, because there is a bad tendency, in the accumulated scholarship and criticism about him, to worry away about where he got his theory about time and duration. Hence we are encouraged to believe that before we read Proust we should find out something about the philosophy of Henri Bergson. But Proust had no philosophical theories worth bothering about. His justly celebrated concern with subjective and objective time is simply the offshoot of his preoccupation with the function of memory, a field of interest in which, we can safely assume, he really was, among great writers, the first cab off the rank. Not even Hamlet complains about how slow his mother was to come upstairs and kiss him, and we may assume that the idea didn't occur to Shakespeare either: not, anyway, as a subject for writing. For Proust, memory is the catalytic theme. Examination of one's own soul was in the air at the time. In Vienna, Arthur Schnitzler, in his fiction, had brought genuinely subtle powers of analysis to the constitution of the human spirit: and had done so rather more plausibly, in fact, than Sigmund Freud, who was also operating in that same period, but who still thought that the fine women of Vienna must have had something wrong with them if they didn't want to sleep with their husbands.

Proust wasn't alone in treating the soul's history as decisive. But he was alone in going back so far, and so deep. The sound of the sea you hear in Proust, as if the whole book were a shell held to your ear, is the sound of the amniotic fluid, reminding you, across all your barriers of self-protection, that the first thing you ever heard was voices in the water. From our viewpoint, his childishness paid off. But for the great artist, everything pays off. That was something Pushkin was terribly right about, in his short time on Earth: for the poet, even the disasters are on the agenda.

Perhaps it merely blurs categories to say that the expression of a thought in prose can have a poetry of its own, but in fact poets have always been attracted to the mere sound of phrases lying loose. Tell a poet that Kepler, with his newly improved refracting telescope, observed SN 1604 in Serpentarius and you might get no reaction. But tell the same poet that Kepler studied the geometry of lunar shadows and he might make a note, because the phrase sounds good. There is an interzone between prose and poetry: a porous border where the discursive expression of a thought is rhythmic or resonant enough to take off on its own and enter the area where words and phrases, seemingly in search of one another, combine into a meaning beyond analysis. Prose that deliberately hankers after the status of poetry is likely to be awful, but poetry that harks back to prose has been a feature of English poetry ever since Shakespeare, who decided, probably for theatrical reasons, that the blank verse paragraph was the best way of stating a chain of thought in poetic form. In his plays, after a transitional period in which he allowed the old technique to coexist with the new (John of Gaunt in *Richard II* begins a scene speaking couplets and graduates to blank verse, as if his anguish could no longer brook confinement), Shakespeare used the couplet that he had inherited from Chaucer mainly to clinch scenes, or, within a scene, to allow an actor to transmit a deliberately stilted effect. He might well have asked his actors to speak in couplets throughout the play, but he would probably have died poor. Later on there were attempts, most notably by Dryden, to revive the couplet as a basic theatrical device, but it was too late: Shakespeare (not to forget his brilliant but short-lived predecessor Marlowe, who gave him the idea for the Mighty Line, and gave us a terrific part for Rupert Everett) had changed the game. If Racine had done the same thing, the French might have had a poetic theatre to rival ours. As things happened, they got stuck with the couplet as the best measure of theatrical speaking.

We were set free, although such was the scale of Shakespeare's success that our playwrights ever since, except for the occasional rebel like Christopher Fry or interloper like T. S. Eliot, have usually avoided the poetry that sounds like poetry. The verse paragraph, however, was such a hit that it invaded the field of formal poetry and became the default mode for any poet who had an argument to develop. The more discursive poems of Pope – *An Essay on Man*, for example – were holdouts against that tendency but they suffered cramps as a consequence. Wordsworth's *The Prelude* would not only have been no better had it been written in a set form, it would have had less in it.

But the poet who really picked up the verse paragraph and ran with it was Browning. His dramatic monologue 'Andrea del Sarto' ('So free we seem, so fettered fast we are!') is pure theatre without the encumbrance of a dedicated building. His blank verse paragraphs link one idea to the next with such a conversational flow that they almost persuade you, as you read, that you yourself are speaking them. But there is such a thing as developing your own breakthrough to the point of disaster. Browning's *The Ring and the Book*, his masterpiece in his own eyes, can be spoken aloud only by a maniac. Cacophonous with syntactical trickery, it's a traffic jam pretending to be a NASCAR race, and clear proof that even the most brilliant artist can go berserk if he gets more interested in his means of expression than in what he has to express. I have to concede, however, that exactly the same objection was levelled at Proust. Do something new, do it well, and there will always be people to say that what you have done was too trivial to bother with.

Isn't a blank verse paragraph just a chunk of prose bent around corners after every five beats? Try doing that and you'll not only get lines that don't scan, you'll also get, and all too often, the one effect that you definitely don't want: successive lines that rhyme. As with any other verse form, the apparently informal form of blank verse requires discipline, and it's out of the requirements of discipline that an unexpected thought arrives, and takes you where you didn't realize that you wanted to go. With blank verse the biggest unforeseen opportunities are offered by the enjambment: a technical French word that has never been fully anglicized because not enough people care.

Unless the line ends with a full stop, the enjambment takes the sentence around the corner. The impetus at the beginning of the next line can be used for dramatic effects. Indeed the project will soon die if it isn't. But let's just assume for now that although the blank verse paragraph is a lot harder to handle than it looks, it's worth the effort for the impetus it can give to an argument: and the impetus can even help to conjure an argument into existence, by dint of the most intoxicating thing that practising an art form can do: make you a bit more clever than you ever realized.

There remains the matter of this poem's language. Our word enjambment made it only into this accompanying essay, but the poem itself, a quinzaine of rhapsodies, is dotted with French words throughout. This isn't, I hope, a posturing caprice on my part, but the result of an intractable fact about the English language. A lot of our words concerning social hierarchy, diplomacy, polite behaviour, food, drink, fashion, style and the fine arts all come from the French. Some of them arrived when the Normans invaded England. The French newcomers were, on the whole – and here I speak as someone whose ancestry began in France on both my mother's and my father's side – a bunch of swine. They ruled not only by violence but by their new invention: manners, then as now one of the most daunting codes of supremacy. Since their power was absolute, their names for polite customs became universal, and even today the phrase for one of their more condescending practices, droit du seigneur, is in our language unchanged. So are the words for (and here I list only some of the French-derived English words in my poem) beau monde, hauteur, salon, soirée, bête noire, cliché, ambience and many others. Some of them tend to lose, in the course of time, their italics and accents, but the French spelling remains as is, or as was. (It is quite common for a French word to go out of a specific use in its country of origin but still be used in its superseded sense by us.) Even in recent times, if the French were first to a social or artistic idea, we tended to borrow the word. Used in the poem, a term like belle époque and a word like demimonde were new at the time when Proust was writing his *roman-fleuve*, but we still use them now, and will probably never change them.

English is unlikely to try disguising its borrowed French words in the near future, although the tin-eared reductionism of the Web might strip them of their accents and Americanize their spellings. English has never been afraid of being taken over by a foreign vocabulary. (Today we have office workers talking of the jihad that has been launched against them by the personnel department.) The French, however, have a traditional fear that their language might be taken over by foreign elements, by which they mean English. (Hence their doomed rearguard action against Franglais.) It probably won't happen, because French, as the language of diplomacy, carries too much historically sanctioned prestige: another French–English word. It's far more likely, when it comes to the higher matters of civilization, that the politically ascendant Anglosphere will continue to speak a language which has been, like Russian society under the Czars, decisively and continuously influenced by France. The polite form of English is really camped between two languages: a fact that this poem happens to reflect, although such was not my aim. On the other hand, I deliberately kept any words of conspicuously German–English (kindergarten, ersatz, blitz, lebensraum) out of my picture, so as to keep the tone germane (yet another French–English word). Tone, in poetry, is always a matter of choice. Some would say that a choice of tone is all that poetry is. It gives a partial view, and the best you can hope for is that the part implies the whole. Try to evoke everything at once and you'll be back to saying what babies say when they cry.

Some admirers of *Finnegans Wake* think that Joyce was trying to speak in the language that a baby speaks in the cradle, when it can pronounce all the sounds of any language in the world. (In Proust's dying year, Joyce met him at a party Proust struggled out to attend because he didn't want to disappoint Stravinsky, Diaghilev and Picasso. Yes, those were the days.) They might be right. We can be sure, however, that Proust was trying to speak the language of someone who has come to the end of life, and wants to pass on the summary of his reflections. It was generous of him. He was rich enough never to do a tap of ordinary work, and right until the last moment, when he was at last shut away from the parties and receptions that he loved, he was still having ice-cream and iced beer sent in from the Ritz. In the cork-lined room of his extinction he could have just lain there and taken more time over his breakfast, instead of fighting like a hero to get his masterpiece finished. Luckily for us, he did the unexpected. That some people will do that is the only thing we can be sure of.

Notes

In the following sheaf of notes, I have tried to pick out a few points in this little book that might conceivably lead the reader out into a wider frame of reference later. In other words, the requirement is that they should be fruitful, and not just routinely explanatory: the poem is meant to explain itself. The notes begin with a point in the Introduction and go on from point to point through the poem. They aren't essential to the poem but they do acknowledge, I hope, an essential feature of poetry: that simply because of the concentration that goes into putting it together, it is a source of radiation.

Learning French from Proust

As I eventually discovered, the best way into a reading knowledge of another language is to start with essays, rather than fiction. But much of Proust's novel is like a critical essay anyway. When Niels Bohr arrived in England and wanted to improve the schoolboy English he had learned in Denmark, he went right through *David Copperfield*, dictionary within reach. Bohr was in Cambridge and Manchester while Proust was still getting ready to write his novel, and at first glance it might seem that no two men could be more different. But taken together they are a good demonstration of how science and art can preoccupy the same design of human brain. They even shared the same style of utterance. It notoriously took Bohr many drafts to produce a paper, and even in his conversation he would often express himself with a hesitancy that taxed the patience of his listeners. His excuse? 'I try not to speak more clearly than I can think.' The motto fits Proust. Today we give arts grants to people who ramble on fluently about nothing, but Proust was concerned with the opposite effect.

Reynaldo Hahn's account

In London the singing teacher Ian Adam, until his death in 2007, would always insist that his pupils work away at the same few *chansons* out of the French repertoire until some mastery was attained over the legato line and the intervals. His own teacher had been Maggie Teyte, who was singing in Paris while Proust was alive, and one of his favourite composers was Reynaldo Hahn, especially for his setting of Victor Hugo's *Si mes vers avaient des ailes* (If my verses had wings), the prodigy Hahn's first hit number after he arrived in Paris from Venezuela. Ian used the Maggie Teyte method of making you sing the one song for months on end until you either got it right or went crazy. (In later years I took my revenge by raiding the orientalist imagery of another of his French favourites – *Les roses d'Ispahan*, music by Fauré and words by Leconte de Lisle – for a poem that I called 'The Falcon Growing Old'.) But it wasn't Ian who gave me the story of Hahn, Proust and the rose bush. I probably got that from one of the biographies. A biographical study is usually fated to go out of date no matter how well written, but the George Painter two-volume *Marcel Proust* is a prose achievement on a level with its subject. The student, however, can safely rest content with William C. Carter's more recent *Marcel Proust*, no miracle of style but full of painstakingly researched facts in the recognized American manner. From Carter you will learn that Proust, in 1916, went out at night by taxi to round up the Poulet string quartet and bring them back to play to him in his room. The piece he wanted to hear was César Franck's Quartet in D. The piece was forty-five minutes long and when the players reached the end, at two o'clock in the morning, they jibbed at Proust's request for them to play it again. But he handed each of them a fortune in bills redeemable for gold, and they played it again.

Thomas Mann made notes

More scholarly admirers of Thomas Mann might like to know that he spoke of his admiration for Proust's richness in words and knowledge (*Bewunderung für seinen Reichtum an Worten und Kenntnissen*) in *Tagebücher* 1937–1939, p.161, with particular reference to Proust's gift for finding in nature the model of his exact observation of the human world.

Like Renoir's La Loge

When I got to London in the early 1960s, this wonderful picture still hung in the old Bloomsbury location of the Courtauld collection, where I could see it every day during my lunch hour. It was painted in 1874 in the fabulously productive period when Renoir was still at the height of his confidence, before Degas scared him back to school and into the stiffness of his *manière aigre*, which he later overcompensated for by turning out lashings of odalisques spun from sugar. Renoir spent little time at the opera. The artists no longer needed the good opinion of high society; but the penalty for freedom was that they sometimes were too dependent on the good opinion of each other. It probably never occurred to Renoir that Degas might have been deliberately trying to mess with his head.

Best reported by Colette

Readers who decide, perhaps quite sensibly, that Proust might be just too much time and trouble, can get a more readily appreciable picture of Paris in those years from the novels of Colette, especially from the *Chéri* novels and most particularly, in my view, from *Julie de Carneilhan*, perfectly translated after World War II by Patrick Leigh Fermor. When the guns went silent in 1945, those among the cultivated young British literary gentry who had survived were generously determined to help transmit the heritage of civilized achievement to the next generation, and there was suddenly a wave of highly competent translation: all the key novels of Colette, for example, were done again in English of an appropriately neat finish and sensitivity to the historical background. Some of the same translators did a similar favour for the small but classic novels of the French nineteenth century, including Alphonse Daudet's *Sappho*, mentioned in the poem. Another must is *Bel Ami*, by Guy de Maupassant. It was out of this 'impulse to preserve', as Philip Larkin put it, that Terence Kilmartin and D. J. Enright found their motivation to complete the Scott Moncrieff translation of Proust.

Bergotte and Elstir

Of the two giant artistic figures in the poem, Bergotte was based on Anatole France and several other writers including Proust himself; and Elstir was based on several painters including perhaps Whistler, whose name is thought by some scholars to have provided the anagrammatic materials for Elstir's. Proust says in *Time Regained* that Marcel, in composing his novel, mixes originals together to form characters in the same way that Françoise mixes various kinds of meat into her famous *boeuf mode*. We should take Proust's word for it. Although nothing will ever stop the scholarly hunt for Proust's points of origin in the real world, it can't be said often enough that he, like all novelists, developed each of his characters by synthesizing the characteristics of several models. It's just that he did even more of that than anyone had done before. The drawback of the method, of course, is that instead of being challenged to a duel by one person when the book comes out, you might be sued into bankruptcy by several.

Laure Hayman

In view of the caveat in the immediately preceding note, Laure Hayman is a scarily relevant case. After the war, when Proust published the second volume of his sequence, Laure Hayman suddenly reminded Proust that she was still very much alive, and as angry as spit. Proust correctly said that he had based his upward-climbing Odette on half a dozen different women, but he was unable to explain why he had equipped Odette with Laure's postal address. Today, she would have been able to stop the book. Early in my career an American friend who subsequently became one of my publishers, Starling Lawrence of Norton, explained to me why his libel lawyers took such pains when vetting a new manuscript: 'Nobody makes anything up.'

The Value of the Ruins

I used this phrase as the title for a section of my poem in a deliberate attempt to save the idea that it contains from being tied irredeemably to the ambitions of Albert Speer. Persuading Hitler that Nazi ceremonial buildings should be constructed solidly enough so that their ruins would still be impressive in a thousand years, Speer risked Hitler's wrath at the implied suggestion that the Third Reich might not last forever. But Speer had chosen his man well: Hitler, essentially a performer, loved the idea, which Speer in his numerous writings called the theory of ruin value (*Die Ruinenwerttheorie*). Luckily very little of what Hitler and Speer planned together ever got built, but the phrase is too good to be consigned to oblivion along with their dreams. The phrase does, after all, have something to it: the Egyptian pyramids and the Sphinx probably look better now than they ever did, and, unless you think they were built by visiting spacemen, the value of their ruins teaches us permanent lessons about human capacities and ambitions.

Cocteau and the Gestapo

Cocteau's spiritual decline after World War II might not have been all to do with drugs. He could have been recalling the shame of having been suckered by the Nazi Occupation of Paris. The Nazi in charge,

Otto Abetz, was billed as the German ambassador to Vichy France, but he was in fact a Francophile SS *Obersturmbannführer* given a special and unusual brief to go easy on the locals. Hence the relatively civilized air of the Occupation, which was such a smooth confidence trick that the French, after the war, were several decades facing up to the full implications of how their collaboration had been secured. With few exceptions, the whole non-Jewish intelligentsia of Paris were able to pursue their careers at the price of carefully not noticing when the people who were Jewish were rounded up and shipped out. I tried to give an account of the subsequent moral shame in my book *Cultural Amnesia*, and I wouldn't want to try presenting a capsule version of the story here. It can't really be encapsulated, because in its full and dreadful subtlety it's the most important story that all the world's intellectuals who have been born since most need to hear. Sufficient to say, perhaps, that although the city that Proust had loved was left looking unchanged after the Nazis went home it had, in sad fact, changed profoundly. Its heart had been broken, and when the heart breaks the mind reels.

Boldini and Whistler

Boldini often spoiled his portraits of fashionable women by overdoing the elongation, so that the would-be elegant distortions rivalled those of Parmigianino and El Greco; but his portraits of fashionable men could be less unlikely. Whistler, however, was more tied to reality no matter whom he painted. The poem is right to say that Whistler never did paint Montesquiou in his notorious white suit, but as Adam Gopnik reminded me (I was ashamed to need reminding, but Proust was right about the community of minds: you can't remember everything all on your own) Whistler did paint Montesquiou in black evening dress, and the portrait, which now hangs in the Frick collection in New York, is quite a thing. Even a whole hundred years later, no great painter courts belittlement quite like Whistler: that defiantly dainty butterfly signature of his was branded by the nervously butch press deep into his cheek. What Whistler gives us, with his young ladies in their frilled white dresses, was the way that the privileged children actually looked. It's a nice question whether the Paris of the belle époque did more to Frenchify his taste than it did to Sargent, whose lastingly famous *Madame X*, she of the knife-like nose and the mind-bending décolletage, could be a grand dame bred to the Faubourg, though she was actually an American married to a French banker. The painting had an unforeseen effect: Sargent had aimed it at the French upper-class market but it wrecked his chances, because none of the French female socialites would have considered showing that much skin. The great ladies were as conservative as Madame de Pompadour: the very thing that Proust loved about them.

His critic Jean-François Revel

Second only to Raymond Aron as a political commentator and critic in the later part of the twentieth century, the formidably cultivated and brilliantly aphoristic Revel – he was a career philosopher until he decided that the philosophers weren't interested enough in being wise – wrote a little book on Proust which anyone who wants to read Proust in the original might consult on the way in. The first merit of Revel's approach is that he has no patience with the notion that Proust's novel might have had a structure. What has a structure in Proust is the thought. The same point is made by Charles Dantzig in his unnervingly brilliant *Dictionnaire égoïste de la littérature française*, in which Proust not only has a dazzling chapter to himself, but is cited to great effect throughout.

Who dined at Magny's

The Goncourt brothers set themselves the task of writing down and abridging all the conversations between literary stars that took place at their table. It was the clearest possible sign that nineteenth-century France had finally caught up with eighteenth-century England, and that the fashionable salons were no longer the most desirable field of operations for the artists, although even in my time in London there were still instances of famous writers, usually visiting Americans such as Gore Vidal and Tennessee Williams, who could manage to spend as much time at the tables of fashionable hostesses as with each other. The two desires are not mutually exclusive. But the preponderance has shifted, and in Paris the shift had already begun before Proust came on the scene. For anyone who wou)ld like to flash back to the sheer excitement generated by the artists and intellectuals starting a new high society of their own – it could be called the upper bohemia – Robert Baldick's book *Dinner at Magny's* (1971) can still be recommended as the classic account, although a more direct approach to Proust's time, which came later, can be made through Roger Shattuck's marvellous cultural study *The Banquet Years* (1969), an exemplary and unrepeatable tour de force in bringing the artistic ferment of the belle époque back to its scintillating life.

Elisabeth, Comtesse Greffulhe

Though the original was almost certainly a much nicer person than the character, this was the aristocratic high priestess who provided the style, class and poise – what would nowadays be called the *look* – of the Duchesse Oriane de Guermantes. The photographs of her are sufficiently impressive, although she never sat for one of the name portrait painters. What she really needed, to do her justice in all three dimensions, was a sculpture by Troubetzkoy, but when outside Russia he mainly busied himself at the service of the emergent American plutocracy. For the Vanderbilts he immortalized every female in the family. Troubetzkoy gets a mention towards the end of the poem but he can only be treated as incidental to the main Parisian action: a great pity for anyone enchanted by his combination of elegance and energy. (George Bernard Shaw was: he commissioned a portrait bust, with a result that leaves the busts by Rodin and Epstein looking, respectively, limp and strained.) A sensitive Marxist analysis, were such a thing possible, might say that Proust's portrait of the Comtesse Greffuhle was a last bourgeois salute, nostalgically romanticized, to the figure of the aristocratic great lady as she disappeared from history. Certainly some such gesture was a universal theme at the time. The Feldmarschallin in *Der Rosenkavalier*, by Richard Strauss and Hugo von Hofmannsthal, first took the stage in Dresden in 1911, under the direction of Max Reinhardt: though she did not reach Paris until 1927, after Proust's death.

Liebestod

The only German word in the poem, apart from *Zeppelin, Gotha, Gestapo, Wehrmacht* and *Die Zeit*. But Wagner was begging to be brought in, because Proust loved his music, which had already had a pervasive effect on any serious music written in France. In Proust's later years there was a system by which performances at the opera house were transmitted over the telephone, so that Proust, scarcely believably, could listen in as he lay ill.

The Duke's novels

The phrase 'worthy of his grocer' is a direct translation. Less than sixty years later, a grocer's daughter would become Prime Minister of Great Britain. But then, well before the Duke's time a military recruit from a very minor and impecunious family of Corsican nobility had become Emperor of France. In that regard, Proust was out of date.

The Face of Dior

My use of product endorsements is meant to be a reference to Proust's celebrated formulation that when we attain a certain degree of knowledge we can get as much information out of a soap advertisement as out of a *pensée* by Pascal.

The Amalienburg

There is much exquisite architecture in Paris but it never hurts to be reminded that some of the really sensational stuff is elsewhere in Europe, often put there because other people have been energized by the spirit of emulation. Just outside Munich, the Nymphenburg Palace of the Wittelsbachs, once the ruling house of Bavaria, would scarcely be worth visiting for the collection of portraits of Ludwig I's girlfriends, but in the garden of the palace the little pavilion called the Amalienburg is one of the most beautiful buildings in the world: a rococo bubble of glass, gold and silver that might leave you thinking again about whether Frank Gehry is really all that original. The pavilion's architect, François de Cuvilliés, was a dwarf: an interestingly visible example of the usually hidden fact that great artists are nearly always unfitted for ordinary society. Proust was no misfit, but he was very sick. Had he been well, he would almost certainly not have written his great novel.

The bronzes of Capo Riace

The Greek bronzes were brought up from the sea floor in 1972 but needed nine years of restoration before they went on display. They are now in the classical museum in Reggio Calabria.

Drancy velodrome

This was the first appearance in modern history of the sports arena in its other role as a holding pen preparatory to kidnap, torture and death. The Jews sat there waiting to be allotted to the trains running east. If Proust had been born healthy, he might have been sitting there too. He would have been an old man by then, but the Nazis, when it came to the important business of exterminating the innocent, were no respecters of age.

Jewess of the high-born bourgeoisie

Her name was Mrs E. Levin and her portrait drawing is one of the most strikingly noble things ever done by Leonid Pasternak, right up there with his portraits of Rilke and Einstein and of his son, Boris. The Mrs Levin portrait of 1916 can be found on the image page of his Google entry, but until recent times, because it was locked up in the Soviet Union, it scarcely registered in modern art history. (The Web is changing the past as well as the future.) Before the Web came into being, the Mrs Levin portrait did feature in a monograph on Pasternak's art that the Soviets published in Moscow in 1975. I bought a copy in London, noted the presence of the bourgeois portrait subjects, and began to arrive at the conclusion that the rewriting of art history by the Soviets had come to a halt and might even be going into reverse. This impression was confirmed a few years later when a two-volume edition of Diaghilev's critical writings was published in Moscow: an essential document for the study of Diaghilev, and sufficient reason all on its own for learning to read Russian. A richly illustrated one-volume condensation of Diaghilev's magazine *Mir Iskusstva* (The World of Art) duly followed. With all this belated truth-telling in train, it was therefore no surprise when the Kremlin softened its ideological strictures, although nobody should be trusted who says that they foresaw the complete collapse of the regime. To retroactively assure us that some event was inevitable is a clear case of predicting the past, an intellectual habit that needs to be avoided. All that aside, however, the presence of Diaghilev's Russian ballet companies in Proust's Paris was stunning early evidence that in the long run artistic imperialism would outrank military imperialism as a measure of national vitality.

She was a born vamp and grew accustomed quite early in her life to carving a path through men. Her immortal love affair with Modigliani happened in Paris in Proust's time. With Akhmatova standing at six feet in height and Modigliani a whole foot shorter, they must have been a striking couple; but neither of them was daunted by the discrepancy, and Modigliani went on drawing her one way or another for the rest of his life. Back in Russia, and unwisely reluctant to leave after the Revolution – the young poets of Petersburg, renamed Leningrad, touchingly believed that the burgeoning creativity of their beautiful city could only flourish further, now that despotism was a thing of the past – Akhmatova went on fascinating men, but when the new regime framed and murdered her poet husband Gumilev she was given an early sign that the new absolutism was going to leave the old one looking like freedom. History made the born vamp into a heroine of the independent spirit, but it was a cruel restriction: she was meant to write her poems about what Nadezhda Mandelstam called 'the privilege of ordinary heartbreaks', not about hell on earth.

Such was Akhmatova's stature, and the accidental confinement of her fame to the borders of her unlucky country, that her name, in my view, should be given its correct pronunciation, with the accent on the second syllable, as the scansion demands when she appears in this poem. The dancer Pavlova's name should have been stressed on the first syllable but when she came to the West nobody could manage it. Something similar recently happened to the tennis champion Maria Sharapova, whose name should be stressed on the second syllable, which would even make it easier to say: but none of our sports commentators could ever manage it, and really there's no point protesting; after all, she was brought up as an American, not as a Russian. The name Pasternak we stress on the first syllable; or else, if we are being fancy and foreign-sounding, on the second; but in fact it should be stressed on the third, just as Nabokov, which we stress on the first, should be stressed on the second. But we in the West are always insistent on doing things our way. Akhmatova, however, belongs to Russia, the eternal Russia. She is theirs before she is ours. Her name should be left as it is, while the Russians get set to resume, if they do, the globally important cultural position that they lost in 1917, in Proust's time.

Gate of Lilacs

Even today, to glance at a map of Paris and see the name Porte des Lilas is enough to take me back to my very first day in the city, when I saw the pictures – the actual pictures this time, not just reproductions – of the Impressionists, who in those days were still in the Jeu de Paume: a more congenial display space for their art, in my belief, than the Musée d'Orsay where they hang now, like prisoners too frail in a fortress far too strong. 'Lilacs' is the word that gives me Paris, in the way that the madeleine gave Proust his childhood memories. The Closerie des Lilas on Montparnasse was a hangout for Hemingway, whose name is still enshrined on a plaque in the piano bar; and it was at the same brasserie that the Dada movement came to an end when André Breton and Tristan Tzara had a fight there in 1922, the very year of Proust's death. As Julian Barnes records in his feast of a book about painting, *Keeping an Eye Open*, Manet, when already dying in the agonies of tertiary syphilis, painted a crystal vase of lilacs: an image of evanescence almost too beautiful to bear.

Ashes of Maria Callas

Feeling determines everything in poetry, even its intellectual themes, and I felt that the great soprano belonged in this poem about Proust because one of the arias she sang in her post-career concerts, the recordings of which I followed closely, was the sumptuous 'Depuis le jour', from Charpentier's belle-époque opera *Louise*. A survey of the YouTube collection of her performances of the aria proves that she sang it from the very beginning of her career, and until the end she went on deepening her interpretation even as her voice became less and less lovely in itself: an heroic arc of dedicated artistry. Charpentier was the son of a baker and he wrote *Louise* – the libretto was largely his too – just in time to catch the turn of the century. It was premiered in Paris in 1900, and was a huge hit. The texture of the music was drawn from the old street cries of Paris, a provenance to which Proust's friend Reynaldo Hahn was sympathetic. But Proust was too much of a Wagnerian to approve of anything so retrograde, and Marcel speaks of the street-cry tradition disparagingly during one of his many quarrels with Albertine in *The Captive*. Artists could still be snobs in those days, especially about a newcomer up from nowhere. Elsewhere in the same city at the same time, if Picasso hadn't had the courage to admire Le Douanier Rousseau nobody else would have admired him either.

I'll drown my books

From *The Tempest*, Act V Scene 1. Prospero says goodbye.

Ah, soldier

From *Antony and Cleopatra*, last act, last scene. It was T.S. Eliot's favourite moment in the play. When Charmian is on the point of death, she says just these two words, like a long sigh. Proust's sigh was even longer.

* * *

Until the advent of Eliot's short epic *The Waste Land*, it was traditional practice that even the longest poem should be presented, for general consideration, unaccompanied by explanatory notes, and be sent forth to posterity that way. There are gifted poets who have written epics that have died in their own lifetime because of their freight of explanatory apparatus: *In Parenthesis*, by the Welsh poet David Jones, was a good, or bad, example of that. As an evocation of the Great War that was fought out a few miles away while Proust was writing his book, Jones's long poem was not without talent, but it dragged in so many curious references and allusions that the reader was soon left without patience. Fighting for his life in the mud and blood, Jones, if he had known what Proust was up to, would have thought it criminally frivolous. But under the eye of eternity, Proust is the serious artist and Jones is forgotten. (My friend P. J. O'Rourke, an admirer of *In Parenthesis*, would not agree that Jones has disappeared: but the cruel facts say that he has.) If Jones had been as devoted to the measure of his subject as he thought, he would not have burdened his work with all that obscurity.

Born while Proust was still alive, William Empson was a rare instance of mathematical and verbal talents sharing the same brain. His slim volume of short poems really added up to an epic. Always keen to transmit the poetry that he found in science, he loaded the back of the book with notes explaining the connections he had made between the two fields. Though they will always be of interest to students of aesthetics concerning themselves with where artists get their ideas from, Empson's notes are not always much less bewildering for their obliquity than the poems themselves. But his poetic works got through to posterity without trouble: they were too melodic not to. Nobody except salaried academics would think that there can be no understanding Empson's verse without his own prose gloss, plus, of course, their commentary on his comments. The same is true, indeed, for *The Waste Land*: the notes were always a bit of a joke anyway – Eliot didn't really expect anybody sane to check up on his references to *The Golden Bough* – and to the extent that they are still remembered, they are remembered because they form part of an unforgettable poem's total melody. Later on in his career, Eliot wrote a slightly longer short epic which is by no means without difficulties, but to which he appended no explanatory notes at all. Called *Four Quartets*, it went straight to posterity by the direct route.

Robert Graves, who fought in the same war as David Jones but is still remembered for doing so, was the first poet in modern times to see not only that a poem should explain itself, but to see that explaining itself is what a poem does. In the long run, if the poet is lucky enough to qualify for that, his poem must go forward minus any furniture pointing out its more arcane references and allusions. Those aspects, if they sound good enough, will be taken for granted, and if they don't sound good enough the poem is sunk from the start.

Or such, at any rate, was true until recently. Now everything can go into the Web and stay there until hell freezes over. Some people think that that's what the Web is – hell, frozen over – but there's no gainsaying the awkward fact that the old curse of oblivion, which was at least half a blessing, is no longer operative. Luckily most of the dud poems, and all the dud epics, will arrive in the Web and rest there undisturbed. But for any poem that still does attract posterity's attention there is a deadlier fate waiting than to be forgotten. There is the threat of being explained.

Any poet who loads his work with obliquities, recondite information and putatively impressive flights of synthetic reasoning must now face the frightening possibility that there will be people who, devoting themselves to the study of what he has done, will make a steadier living out of it than he did. On the off-chance that someone in the next generation might go into business as an explainer of my poem about Proust, I have listed above a few of the points that he might begin with. Having noted them first, I might have pre-empted at least part of a potentially superfluous discussion, and thereby helped to stave off a doomed search for my poem's hidden secret.

'My book has no key,' said Proust, and I can say the same for this poem written in his honour. Really what I have done is to mark enough trails so as to lead any such discussion away from myself, and towards the solid topics of art, history, politics and philosophy that all accrue naturally to any discussion of Proust's masterpiece. This is a poem about him, not me; and in fact it is not even about him, but about what he did. After a blessed life as a writer in reasonable health, and having faced no dangers except the consequences of my own folly, all I do in the poem is work my way towards death. Proust does the same, but on the way he writes *A la recherche du temps perdu*. It is a work on which we may comment endlessly, but if, in itself, it really needed our commentary it would never have been great. Explain it all we like, we should never lose sight of the extent to which it explains us, and the death-defying false position we are placed in simply by our will to live. Long before he embarked on the composition of his great novel, Proust wrote a little sketch, never collected into volume form while he was alive, about walking across the Tuileries in late summer. The first leaves of autumn were already on the ground, but it seemed to him that instead of portending winter they merely reflected the golden light of the warm sun: *tout le mirage de l'Imagination, du Regret et du Souvenir.* All the mirage of the Imagination, Regret and Memory. That sad word 'mirage' was his, but the capital letters were his too: tokens of our thirst for splendour, bulwarks against oblivion.